# The Gilbert Collection at Somerset House

Philip Wilson Publishers in association with

The Gilbert Collection

# The Gilbert Collection of Decorative Arts

THE GILBERT COLLECTION was formed over four decades in Los Angeles, California, and is entirely the result of one man's passion for great craftsmanship. In the late 1960s Arthur Gilbert started to collect English silver and Italian mosaics. He was attracted to silver because of its artistry and historical associations and at the same time became fascinated by the painstaking techniques of Roman nineteenth-century micromosaics. From these beginnings the collection has grown to become one of the greatest of its kind in the world. Today it comprises English and European gold and silver, gold snuffboxes, enamel portrait miniatures and mosaics from Florence and Rome. In each of these fields it is pre-eminent.

Arthur Gilbert was born in London in 1913. In 1949 he and his late wife Rosalinde moved to California. There he embarked on a successful career in real estate and started to collect works of art. Like most private collections, his began without any particular plan beyond his own enjoyment. He collected silver to decorate his home and his first micromosaic picture was bought on a whim, because it looked so astonishingly like a painting. Gold snuffboxes developed into an independent field of collecting after he acquired some micromosaic plaques that happened to be fitted into snuffboxes. In a similar way the portrait miniatures collection was an off-shoot from gold boxes.

During the early 1990s, after a long association with the Los Angeles County Museum of Art, Gilbert began looking for a permanent home for his collection and it was at this point that the exciting possibility of Somerset House was first proposed. This great complex of buildings was erected in the late eighteenth century on the site of Protector Somerset's sixteenth-century palace and was designed by George III's architect, Sir William Chambers. It was built to provide offices for the civil service and learned societies. The Royal Academy of Arts occupied the North Block while the South Building, adjacent to the so-called King's Barge House, housed the Navy and Stamp offices. The Barge House, now known as the Embankment Building, was originally

Artist's impressions of the micromosaics collection in the South Building and Indian palace furniture in the Embankment Building. Visuals by Anthony Cowland.

built out into the river and was a gateway onto what was then the most important thoroughfare of the metropolis. But the magnificence of its early days gradually faded. The societies moved elsewhere, the civil service functions were gradually downgraded and the building of the Victoria Embankment in the 1860s cut the building off completely from the river .

A major step in the revival of Somerset House was taken in 1990 with the opening of the Galleries of the Courtauld Institute in the North Block. But it was only with the launching of the Heritage Lottery Fund in the early 1990s that it became possible to extend the process to the rest of the complex. As a result of a series of major grants the task has now been magnificently accomplished. The River Terrace and the Great Court have been restored and reopened to the public and the South Buildings have been completely renovated. In 1996 Arthur Gilbert, captivated by the scale of this vision, gave his collection to the nation and in 1999 his outstanding generosity was recognised by the award of a knighthood in the Queen's Birthday Honours.

The Gilbert Collection is displayed in a series of brilliantly contrasting spaces in the Embankment Building and part of the South Building. The micromosaics and gold boxes are shown in the latter and the Embankment Building, with its superb vaulted spaces and river views, is devoted to the silver and Florentine *pietre dure* collections. A remarkable dividend of the entire project has been the restoration of Chambers' Great Arch in the Embankment Building, the original watergate to Somerset House, at the base of which is displayed an eighteenth-century Navy Commissioners' barge of the kind that would originally have plied the Thames between Somerset House and Greenwich. This very rare survival has been loaned by the National Maritime Museum at Greenwich.

The key to all these initiatives has been the extraordinary gift of the Gilbert Collection, now permanently housed in Somerset House. Many of the most important works in the collection have historic associations with this country and its return to England might therefore be called 'heritage regained'. That it should additionally have been the cause of such a programme of restoration of one of the nation's greatest eighteenth-century buildings makes it nothing less than heritage doubly regained.

# Gold and Silver

THE ART OF THE GOLDSMITH is one of the oldest in the world. Since very early times, vessels of gold and silver have been desirable status symbols in wealthy households. Richly ornamented objects were often made simply for display and as a measure of the taste and power of their owners. Sources as diverse as the Old

## Ewer

Anatolia (Turkey),
c. 2500 BC
Gold

This is one of the earliest gold vessels in the world. Made in Bronze Age Anatolia, in modern-day Turkey, the ewer was raised from a sheet of gold and embossed with a pattern of intersecting ribs. The underneath of the base is chased with a swastika, an ancient symbol of good fortune.

## Casting bottle

London, 1553–54,
indistinct maker's mark
Silver-gilt

Made for sprinkling
scented rosewater through
the pierced screw top, these
very personal items were
common in the sixteenth
century, but are extremely
rare survivors today. Only
three others like this one
are known.

Testament, Norse sagas from Viking times and accounts of
Medieval pageants all testify to the importance of goldsmiths' work
as a backdrop to ceremonial occasions. Diarists and letter-writers
from more recent times show the same tradition continued into the
eighteenth and nineteenth centuries.

The Gilbert Collection contains over 300 works in gold and silver plate. A few items are extraordinarily early survivors, such as an
Anatolian gold ewer from the third millennium BC or a small chalice from the twelfth century AD but most date from the sixteenth to
the nineteenth centuries and provide an exceptionally full picture
of the range and styles of European silver from the Renaissance to
the Victorian era. One of the most distinctive features of the

# Partridge

Nuremberg, Germany,
c. 1600, mark of Jorg Ruel
Silver, silver-gilt, mother-
of-pearl, rubies, emeralds

Many sixteenth-century
German vessels were made
in the form of birds and
animals with detachable
heads. An object as
precious as this would have
been intended purely as a
work of art and would have
had pride of place in a
princely treasury or
*Schatzkammer*.

# Nef

Regensburg, Germany,
c. 1610, maker's mark AP
Silver, silver-gilt, gold
enamel

The word 'nef' comes from
medieval French and refers
to a vessel formed like a
ship, used to mark the place
of the host or guest of
honour at table. This one is
made in the form of a ewer,
with the spout at the front,
but was in all probability
seldom put to practical use.

collection is its focus on fine craftsmanship and it is much richer in ornamental objects than in utilitarian wares. Some, of course, fit both descriptions, such as the Anatolian gold ewer or the 1553 casting bottle. The great ewer and dish and the silver-gilt cup by Paul de Lamerie, however, have the appearance of practical objects but were actually made for display on the sideboard and to enhance the status of their owners. As a result, they remain to this day in pristine condition.

Other pieces in the collection were made as precious works of art. Objects such as a sixteenth-century jewelled mother of pearl partridge or a nef from Regensburg were deliberately made as confections or as a way of displaying natural curiosities of exceptional beauty or rarity.

Another special aspect of the collection, shown in a separate

## Ewer and dish

London, 1742–43, mark of Paul de Lamerie
Silver

One of de Lamerie's most opulent works, this ewer and dish was commissioned by the sixth Earl of Mountrath. The relief scenes on the dish are of Jupiter and Venus, with the riches of the earth and the sea to either side. The watery theme of the ewer is appropriately represented by a relief of Neptune.

# Cup and cover

London, 1742-43, mark of
Paul de Lamerie
Silver-gilt

Probably modelled by the
same anonymous artist as
the great ewer and dish,
this is one of the most
densely decorated of all de
Lamerie's works. The
theme, appropriately
enough, is wine. The
figures on either side
represent the infant
Bacchus, the ancient
Roman god of wine, and
the handles and much of
the other ornament is
composed of vines.

# Lafayette vase

Paris, France, 1830–35,
signed by Jacques-Henri
Fauconnier
Silver-gilt

Marie-Joseph, marquis de
Lafayette (1747–1834) was
a hero of both the French
and American revolutions;
this magnificent vase was
commissioned by the
French national guards to
celebrate his life. The relief
panels represent scenes
from his career and the
figures at each corner of
the base are emblematic of
Liberty, Equality, Strength
and Wisdom.

# Cup and cover

London, 1806–7, mark
of Digby Scott and
Benjamin Smith II
Gold

A special commission for
Sir Robert Wigram, this
cup was given to him by the
London regiment he
commanded. The overall
design is in keeping with
the canons of neoclassical
style, while the cartouche
around the inscription
reflects the military nature
of the commission.

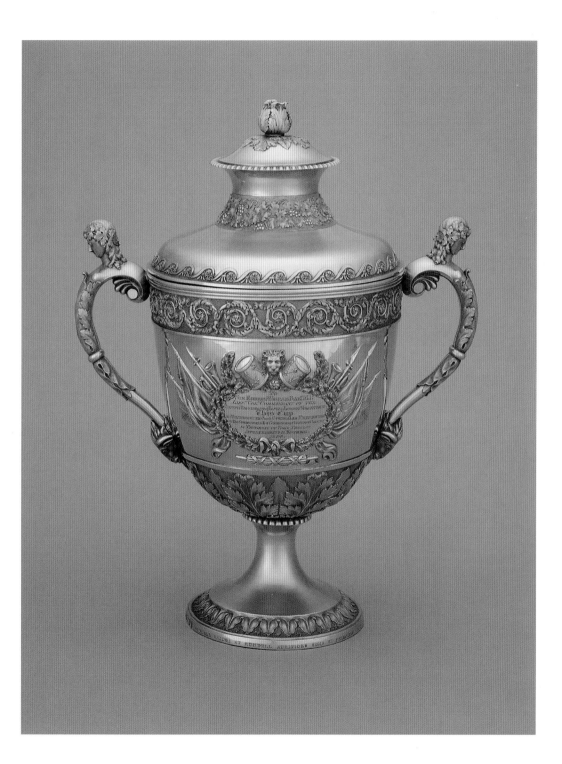

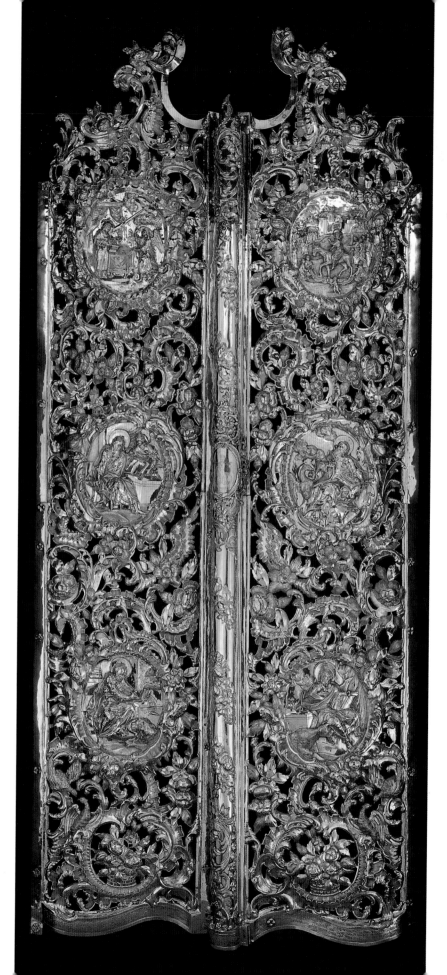

# Pair of royal gates

Kiev, Ukraine, 1784,
attributed to Gregory
Chizhevski
Silver and silver-gilt

This magnificent pair of
gates was presented in 1784
by Catherine the Great to
the monastery of Pechersk
Lavra in Kiev. Kiev was an
important artistic centre in
the eighteenth century and
the gates are among the
finest survivals from this
brilliant period. They
formed the central feature
of the iconostasis, or wall of
icons, which separates the
sanctuary from the nave in
an Orthodox church, and
symbolise the entrance to
the Kingdom of Heaven.
They are called 'royal'
because Christ, the King of
Heaven, passes through
them in the form of the
eucharist.

# Howdah

Rajasthan, India, late
nineteenth century,
no marks
Silver, silver-gilt, wood,
velvet

A howdah is a chair for
riding on an elephant. This
one was made for an Indian
Maharajah and is typical of
the opulence of the
princely courts of India
after Queen Victoria was
proclaimed Empress in
1877.

room in the museum, is the large number of objects made of solid
gold. Gold plate was always rarer and more costly than silver but
from an historical perspective it has a special interest because,
unlike silver, it does not tarnish and for this reason retains the sub-
tle details of finish that are usually lost from silver. The collection
contains no fewer than thirty such pieces (not including the gold
snuffboxes) and is one of the largest accumulations of such material formed in modern times. Among its highlights are the 1806 cup
by Digby Scott and Benjamin Smith and an exquisite late nineteenth-century enamelled gothic revival chalice.

# Chalice

Paris, France, probably late
nineteenth century, no marks
Gold, enamel, pearls, diamonds

The gothic revival was one of the
main styles of the second half of the
nineteenth century. This sumptuous
chalice incorporates brilliant
translucent enamel plaques of the
four evangelists and scenes from the
life of the Virgin. Undoubtedly an
important special commission, the
chalice is not signed and it is not
known by whom or for whom it was
made. The style of the enamels,
however, are strikingly similar to
signed works by the Parisian
goldsmith Lucien Falize.

# Gold Boxes

GOLD BOXES were made as containers for snuff, a form of powdered and scented tobacco that became a craze throughout eighteenth-century Europe. Snuff-taking developed into an elaborate social ritual and gave rise to an entirely new art form of superbly made and very expensive boxes epitomising the luxurious tastes of the aristocracy.

The demand for these precious objects was enormous. London, Berlin and Geneva all became major centres of gold box production, although the most important of all was Paris. Many gentlemen had several boxes appropriate to different occasions or costumes and the writer Louis-Sebastien Mercier even quipped in

## Snuffbox

Paris, France, 1777–79,
mark of
Pierre-Francois Drais
Gold, glazed miniatures,
pearls, enamel

The painted miniature on the cover is by a member of the van Blarenberghe family and illustrates a famous episode in 1740 when the royal stag hounds chased a deer up the roof of a barn.

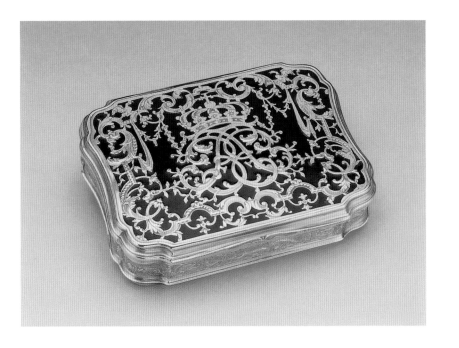

## Snuffbox with portrait of Philip V of Spain

Paris, France, 1717–22, no maker's mark
Gold, tortoiseshell

The monogram on the cover is for Philip V of Spain (1683–1746), whose miniature portrait is inside. Philip was grandson of Louis XIV of France. He was proclaimed King of Spain in 1700 and married Isabella Farnese of Parma in 1714. The box was probably a gift from the king to his wife.

1781 that a properly dressed gentleman should have a different box for every day of the year.

Boxes were often given as intimate personal gifts, much as jewellery was. The early eighteenth-century box with the monogram and portrait of Philip V of Spain was probably a gift from the king to his wife. Snuffboxes also played a role in eighteenth-

# Snuffbox

St. Petersburg, Russia, 1762-66, attributed to Jean-Pierre Ador, no marks
Gold, enamel

This box was made for Baron Nicolaus von Korff (1710–66) and is decorated in enamel with his coat-of-arms and the various medals and orders with which he was presented. On the cover is the Russian Order of St. Andrew and on the front the Prussian Order of the Black Eagle.

# Snuffbox made for Frederick the Great

Berlin, Germany, c. 1765
Gold, mother-of-pearl, precious stones, carved hardstones

The snuffboxes made for Frederick the Great of Prussia (r. 1740–86) are among the most sumptuous and extravagant ever made and were considered to be enormously valuable at the time, containing large diamonds of exceptional quality.

century diplomacy as official gifts to ambassadors, royal servants and foreign heads of state. The services of the English doctor Thomas Dimsdale warranted such a gift from the Russian Empress Catherine the Great; another box with the monogram of her predecessor, Elizabeth I, was probably also a diplomatic offering. They were usually accepted in the spirit of cash presents and

## Box with cypher of Elizabeth I of Russia

Germany, probably
Augsburg or Dresden,
c. 1755
Gold, amethyst, glazed
miniature

Although doubtless commissioned by the Imperial Court in St Petersburg, this box was probably made in Augsburg or Dresden. The initials on the cover are for the Empress Elizabeth Petrovna (1709–62), daughter of Peter the Great. The front of the box is decorated with the device of the Russian Order of St. Andrew and the inside of the cover with a miniature portrait of the Empress.

assessed on the basis of the intrinsic value of their component gold and gemstones, often being sold on soon afterwards.

Gold boxes had an aesthetic importance that went beyond the cost of their materials, however. The best of them display originality of form, decoration and materials and an astonishing virtuosity of craftsmanship, treating on a miniature scale the same styles and subjects as contemporary designs and paintings. Seen as such, they emerge at their best as some of the most remarkable works of art of the eighteenth century and as a microcosm of their age. The Gilbert Collection contains some 220 boxes, comprising as encyclopaedic a presentation of this diverse art form as can be seen anywhere in the world.

The crowning glory of the collection is the group of six magnificent boxes made for Frederick II of Prussia. Frederick, known as 'the Great', ruled Prussia from 1740 until his death in 1786 and turned the country into an eighteenth-century superpower, laying the foundations of modern Germany. Under his regime, Berlin

# Snuffbox with étui, watch and chatelaine

Vienna, Austria, c. 1760, the enamel by Phillip Ernst Schindler II
Gold and enamel

It is rare for such a set to survive together and this is one of the finest
examples of Schindler's sophisticated enamel painting. The étui (on the
left of the group) is fitted with various implements including a small
knife with interchangable gold and steel blades, a snuff spoon, a
toothpick, an ear pick and a pair of scissors.

## Bonbonnière

Dresden, Germany, c. 1780, attributed to Johann Christian Neuber
Gold, hardstone, mosaic

Johann Christian Neuber specialised in gold snuffboxes inlaid with brilliant designs in polished hardstones. This box has been built around two Roman micromosaics, probably by Giacomo Raffaelli, who was one of the pioneers in the development of these highly accomplished miniature works of art.

became a centre of patronage, with artists, musicians and philosophers from all over Europe being attracted to his court.

The area of patronage on which Frederick most clearly left his mark is gold boxes. He had a passion for them and is said to have owned more than 300. Only 26 of the boxes commissioned by Frederick are known to have survived. Apart from the eight preserved at Schloss Charlottenberg in Berlin, the boxes in the Gilbert Collection are the largest group anywhere in the world.

# Florentine Hardstones

THE GILBERT COLLECTION includes two distinct types of mosaics, Roman micromosaics and Florentine hardstone mosaics, or *pietre dure*. The latter date from the sixteenth to the nineteenth centuries and were made of marbles and minerals quarried and collected from around the world. Both forms of mosaic were highly prized as princely gifts and collected by foreign visitors on the Grand Tour.

The hardstones collection, though less extensive than the

## Collector's cabinet

Prague, Bohemia,
c. 1610, Castrucci
Workshop
Hardstones, ebonised and
gilded wood

*Pietre dure*, or hardstone mosaics, were so admired by the Holy Roman Emperor Rudolph II (d. 1612) that in 1588 he established his own imperial workshop in Prague. The workshop was run by the Florentine Castrucci family, famous for their landscapes in subtly hued stones.

## Clock

Rome, Italy, Giacomo
Raffaelli, 1804
Hardstones, micromosaic,
Gilt-bronze

Given by Pope Pius VII to
Napoleon on the occasion
of his coronation in 1804.
It resonates with Imperial
symbolism – images of
Mars (the Roman God
of War), Victory and
righteous conflict adorn
the clock which is designed
in the form of a triumphal
arch.

## Clock cabinet

Florence, Italy, Grand
Ducal workshops, probably
Giovanni Battista Foggini;
(lower cabinet: nineteenth
century)
Hardstones, mother-of-
pearl, ebonised oak, gilt-
metal

The upper section is one of
the most spectacular
products of the Grand
Ducal workshops and is
brilliantly carved with relief
decoration. The lower
cabinet was made over a
hundred years later in
Florence, but bears a
spectacular *trompe l'oeil*
central panel probably
originally from a casket of
about 1700.

# Parure

Naples, Italy, c. 1808, Real Laboratorio
Hardstones, gold

A parure is a matched set of jewellery, in this case consisting of a comb, tiara, necklace and a pair of earrings. At the end of the eighteenth century, under Napoleonic rule, the royal workshop in Naples produced jewellery to the same designs as those from the *Opificio delle Pietre Dure* in Florence. This set originally belonged to Napoleon's sister, Caroline Murat, Queen of Naples.

micromosaics, covers a broader period, ranging from seventeenth-century objects made under the patronage of the Grand Dukes of Tuscany, to late nineteenth-century pictures by the Montelatici family workshop, which is still in business today. The cut and polished hardstones inlaid in wood and marble make up the colourful surfaces of cabinets, tables, clocks and pictures in the Gilbert Collection.

*Pietre dure* objects were coveted by many European rulers. We do not know who commissioned one of the earliest objects in the collection, The Baptism of Christ painted on amethyst by Filippo Lauri, but the taste of the Holy Roman Emperor Rudolph II (d. 1612) is exemplified by the collector's cabinet made under his patronage at the imperial workshop in Prague by the Florentine Castrucci family. In the eighteenth century, English grand tourists visited Florence and collected hardstone cabinets and tables for their country houses. With the nineteenth-century international industrial arts exhibitions, the popularity of Florentine hardstone mosaics grew and a broad spectrum of people including tourists to Italy, designers and collectors acquired hardstones in the Grand Ducal tradition.

Sir Arthur Gilbert began collecting hardstone mosaics in parallel with his quest for Roman micromosaics. He was fascinated by the superlative designs, brilliant natural colours and the amazing capacity for polished stones to appear like the surface of a painting or even a three-dimensional object. These two distinct areas of the collection provide opportunities to compare the techniques and materials of the differing mosaics.

# Roman Micromosaics

Sir Arthur Gilbert's collection of Roman micromosaics grew out of his sheer delight in the remarkable technique behind pictures that at first glance appear to be paintings but on closer inspection reveal their true identity as mosaics made from tiny pieces of opaque glass known as 'tesserae'. It was purely by chance that he discovered a micromosaic picture at a local auction house in Los Angeles, and his fascination with the medium developed into a quest to learn as much as possible about the techniques,

## Table with Apollo

Probably Rome, Italy,
c. 1880–90
Micromosaic, gilt-bronze

This is the only known table entirely covered with micromosaics and shows Apollo in his chariot pulled by four white horses.

## Pair of vases

Rome, Italy, c. 1795–1800,
Nicola de Vecchis (d. 1834)
Marble, hardstone,
micromosaic

This extraordinary pair of vases was once owned by Empress Josephine at Malmaison and was amongst the gifts brought from Rome by Pope Pius VII for the coronation of Napoleon in 1804. They are the earliest known examples of micromosacis executed on a curved surface.

craftsmen and patrons of micromosaics. Over the last thirty years, Sir Arthur has built a collection of over 200 micromosaic objects, including examples from France, Russia, and Italy, made between the sixteenth and the twentieth centuries. However, the vast majority of the collection was made in Rome in the late eighteenth and nineteenth centuries. Like other areas of the Gilbert Collection, it is pre-eminent in its field, comparable only to the Hermitage in St. Petersburg and the Vatican Museum in Rome.

The Gilbert Collection's micromosaics range from large pictures and tables containing tens of thousands of tesserae, to jewels, snuffboxes and small plaquettes of incredibly fine detail. The earliest is a Venetian mosaic of 1566, made to decorate St Mark's Basilica in Venice, already a famous glassmaking centre. In the early eighteenth century, Roman chemists at the Vatican Mosaic Workshop developed the matt opaque coloured glass-like material called 'smalti', of which micromosaics are composed, in contrast to the transparent shiny glass from Venice.

The Vatican Mosaic Workshop's micromosaics became popular as impressive diplomatic presentation pieces. For Napoleon's coronation, Pope Pius VII solicited the advice of Antonio Canova, Italy's foremost sculptor, to select appropriate gifts. Amongst these was the Gilbert Collection's magnificent hardstone clock with micromosaic plaques by Giacomo Raffaelli, one of the first mosaic artists to perfect the technique of *mosaico in piccolo* (mosaic in miniature). Tsar Nicholas I was an avid collector of micromosaics and gave numerous commissions to the foremost mosaicist of the nineteenth century, Michelangelo Barberi, whose magnificent tables dominate the mid-nineteenth-century mosaics in the Gilbert Collection.

Other micromosaics in the collection were produced by the multitude of private workshops established in response to tourism after the Napoleonic Wars. The volume of micromosaic work reflected the popular fashion for the antique, generating a lucrative market for souvenirs of Rome.

# Tigress

Venice, c. 1850, Decio Podio
Micromosaic

Micromosaics were often based on earlier paintings like
this one after the Tigress Lying Below Rocks by George
Stubbs (1724–1806). The tiger was a gift from Lord Clive,
Governor of Bengal, to the fourth Duke of Marlborough
for his menagerie at Blenheim Palace. The painting
commissioned by the duke was copied in prints which
served as the model for this mosaic picture.

# Portrait Miniatures

THE ENAMEL PORTRAIT MINIATURES include some of the most recently acquired objects in the Gilbert Collection. Sir Arthur's interest in them developed as an extension of the collection of gold boxes, in which portrait miniatures were often mounted. The miniatures portray numerous significant historical subjects, often connected by provenance with other objects in the collection.

## The First Duke of Marlborough

England, c. 1705–10,
Charles Boit (1662–1727)
Enamel with silver-gilt
frame

The Swedish enameller
Charles Boit was a key
figure in the development
of the enamel portrait
miniature in England.
He moved to England in
1687 and became Court
enameller to William III.

## Queen Charlotte

London, 1781, Johann
Heinrich Hurter (1734–99)
Enamel, gold-rim frame,
pearls, rubies

When Queen Charlotte arrived
from Germany as consort to
George III in 1761 she created
the Royal appointment of
Miniature Painter. Not only
was the Queen fond of
miniatures, she was also a
popular subject for other
artists. This portrait by Johann
Heinrich Hurter, a Swiss
enameller, is a copy from
Gainsborough's famous
portrait which is still in the
Royal Collection.

Portrait miniatures in enamel were popular from the seventeenth to the nineteenth centuries as objects for personal adornment, for display in a collector's cabinet, or even framed and hung on a wall together with small paintings. Enamel miniatures became fashionable in Switzerland and France in the late seventeenth century because of the permanence and brilliance of the medium. Immigrant artists such as Charles Boit and Christian Friedrich Zincke worked in England in the eighteenth century and trained younger studio assistants, fostering a tradition of enamelling that endured throughout the nineteenth century. Many of the early enamellers came from a background of jewellery-making or goldsmithing.

Patrons and sitters included members of the ruling houses of Europe as well as wealthy merchants, clergymen or lawyers. In the nineteenth century, the popular enameller Henry Bone painted from life as well as copying historical portraits in larger formats.

# George Washington

England, 1825
Henry Bone (1755–1834)
after Gilbert Stuart
(1755–1828)
Enamel on copper

The enameller Henry
Bone specialised in copies
after full-scale paintings.
He experimented with
enamelling techniques
and made large plaques
like this version of
George Washington.
Bone inscribed detailed
information about the
original painting by
Gilbert Stuart and the kiln
firing of this plaque.

Hung in wooden or gilded frames on a wall of a display closet or cabinet, these were known as cabinet miniatures.

The Gilbert Collection contains approximately 80 portrait miniatures, in addition to many more set into gold boxes. The majority of the collection depicts British subjects, some painted by Continental artists working in England. Leading Swiss and French miniaturists, such as Jean Petitot and Jean-François Favre, are also represented, as well as artists from the German, Scandinavian and Russian schools.

Text and illustrations © 2000 The Gilbert Collection
Designed by Peter Campbell
Printed and bound in Italy by
Società Editoriale Lloyd, Srl, Trieste

**Heritage Lottery Fund**

This publication has been made possible by
a grant from the Heritage Lottery Fund.